T0316788

THE PORCH IS A JOURNEY DIFFERENT FROM THE HOUSE

New Issues Poetry & Prose

Editor	Herbert Scott
Copy Editors	Eric Hansen, Derek Pollard, Jonathan Pugh
Readers	Kirsten Hemmy, Adela Najarro, Margaret von Steinen, Cody Todd
Assistants to the Editor	Rebecca Beech, Lynnea Page, Marianne E. Swierenga
Business Manager	Michele McLaughlin
Fiscal Officer	Marilyn Rowe

New Issues Poetry & Prose
The College of Arts and Sciences
Western Michigan University
Kalamazoo, MI 49008

An Inland Seas Poetry Book

 Inland Seas poetry books are supported by a grant from
The Michigan Council for Arts and Cultural Affairs.

First Edition, 2004.

ISBN	1-930974-36-1 (paperbound)

Library of Congress Cataloging-in-Publication Data:
Saskya, Ever
The Porch is a Journey Different From the House/Ever Saskya
Library of Congress Control Number: 2003104654

Art Director	Tricia Hennessy
Designer	Jesse Frein
Production Manager	Paul Sizer
	The Design Center, Department of Art
	College of Fine Arts
	Western Michigan University

THE PORCH IS A JOURNEY DIFFERENT FROM THE HOUSE

EVER SASKYA

New Issues

WESTERN MICHIGAN UNIVERSITY

Ever Saskya's journey is mapped in a book of delightful signs that circulate and spin meanings rather paradoxically. It is a search for personal, aesthetic and historical grounds; the spaced typographies recall Mallarmé as the poet steers through the future of lyric. Addresses to the reader, through the reader, energize this text; many poems inventively collage scientific, theoretical, and poetic information in challenging ways.
　　　　　　　—Brenda Hillman

to Albert and Martha Haynes

Contents

Acknowledgments

Grateful acknowledgement is made to Western Michigan University's Women's Studies, Africana Studies, and American Studies departments for the grant of scholarship, which enabled me to work on this book. I also wish to acknowledge the following people for supporting my work and process: Richard Jackson, Earl Braggs, Ken Smith, Herb Scott, Gwen Raaberg, Gail Landberg, Patty Deloach (DJD), Ben Wilson (Pa), Liz Foster, and Jim McKnew.

A story has no beginning or end; arbitrarily one chooses that moment of experience from which to look back or from which to look ahead.
—Graham Greene

Text

Read T H U N D E R

Refrigerate
the stars, other planets,

light going into dated apple orchards,

distinguish Jupiter from Mars
by sounds from our mouths.

As if eternity held

directions for a telescope:

1.←—)ʃʃ— ⌐ ⟩ᴧ_ ∨⟩⌐ᴧ ⏌_ᴧ _ᴧ
2.←—⌐⏌ _⏌ II∨√IᴎN II_IᴎI⟩ ᴎ _ʃ
3. _⏌ _ᴧ ʃ∨⏌ ⟩⌐ᴧ_ ←_)ʃ _√⌐ ∨ʃΣ⏌
4._ ⌐→⟩ ᴧ_ʃ√IIN ᴎ ∨⌐ʃᴧII⌐⟩ ⟩ ⏌_⟩

My father could not read
1, 2, 3, or 4

the words
a chamber of lines.

His eyes over diagrams

read stars into being.

Memories of their names,
positioning hard light,
until the shore of another
rose in nebulae—

burgundy
night violet.

The scent of light
was Jupiter, the fragrance
of inlaid eves.

Here there were no cards
to be played or signed,
no letters to write or read.

Words,
and the world
on fire for nothing?

A casting of lines
to reach and retrieve him

words like l i f e:
coming in the copse
spreading out
under long dreads of grass,

then spelling
Autumn correctly.

And to the time I showed father Duncan
under Du
and not De in the phonebook

(And to any reader)
I want to tell

he could make the letter A
with lights from the field. Words in the sky,
our night, a waiting text—

always there is more
beyond what telescopes can see.

§ This is the Laubach Reading Program:

And I have nothing new
to tell the world

history
is how we exchange ourselves.

And this is my father. Say *father,*
who cannot read.

This is my father, who
can say *moon.* The moon itself
can settle in the woods
behind the shape of an O.

This is the shutting off of light
before it comes from the moon. Say
illiteracy.

Reading? This
is opening
the door wide
under a half moon (almost forming
the letter D)

nothing like the sun spreading the scent
of lemon grass. This is a field
of stars.

This is the way the moon
is pronounced
in a field
of stars: *moooooooooooon.*

No one needs
to say anything;

light shows the grass has faded after evening.

Yellow exchanged for purple in a painting
can represent night, life-fire, a hand adjusting
a telescope.

Forget the scent of lemon grass (even you and I
can read) under the galaxy

of fruit and May apples
pruned from the field,

as if winter held
the sound of the letters
l
i
f
e
as thunder.

The sound of the letters
t
h
u
n
d
e
r
again again again
coming in the stratus, rolling in on night
as it fires.

My father
can read thunder,

just not like you and I read
thunder.

authenticate • automatic autograph

notice
the backyard swing set held wireless
inside gravity—

the sky position—holds everything
and everyone here for now.

Make that fair by unpacking
suitcases of history—

we never match existence.

Essence is pulled-out-pollen
turned through napalm-flower

—read it as it lives—

Napoleon

touches him, walks grass
off the shoulder, horse-
back-bones, the roll

over humps the back—

humpbacks can be P's or whales
(an individual afflicted).

Anything formed to this left
can be copied

out of the clay of language
the mind lettering:

Christopher Columbus

One gram of bark in collapse—enough
to carve the letter *I*
as birds break into an Evensong
—present is *plume* (feather)
pen   *coup de plume* (feather blow)—

gravity holds everything
and everyone here for now—

rolls our humped backs,
individual afflictions.

What can be done
with our hands (never match

existence
for existence).

Thieves

I have avoided the changing lanes and guns
uncovered
among the dam of library books

(this is not the problem).

I chose
a picture of burlap
over hands dissembled,   lattice of bone   intertwined.

Researched
our misery   others

described in the poem,
for *others*
who buy the book.

The lens (person behind the camera)
first eyed the event
folded   boxed   blanket
cover over—a daughter   broken apart by a landslide.

Eventually,
the *world*—will see it brought into
capitalism—will not find out

how we have exchanged
someone's feet for another's:
devour relief maps (well traveled with

another's habits-less-evil—our history
not becoming war enough)

that lace Diaspora

as feet shed movements
of parting Latvians—

dust blown apart
through the feet of men.

Steal anyone   any horrible

adjective
for adjective

whose death can be written about   that *someone*
will want to read?

Miners in West Virginia

We will never forget that moment on the grounds
when the ruffed men stood still, then turned like ghosts.
And we were there, and sitting still
heard the hang-arounds enter the darkness. Suspending
their last moment, before truth hunts itself.

But that day passed with the trains
and all night we watched men huddle in their coats,
push more paper into barrels, stirring, they seemed
not to bother with us
and we stayed watching.

I, in my coat,
thinking: *The stones rolling away and the air thrust*
Into the lung of a cave . . .

We moved around them, among them, and nothing happened.
A while passed, more arrived,
we came to a large water tower—
the city constantly pushed dirt there.

Then wagons came, along with them piles
of jacked trees and finally an ambulance—
the digging went on for hours.

Few were pulled out. Others waited, while
some were radished from the ground by shovels,
stacked inside trucks, leftover miracles
reached toward other hands.

Were they never told the ways of anaphora? They will be born
a town's distance from the mouth; they will be born
as thrust for the lungs of a cave.

More will come tomorrow, crumpled in their coats,
clinging to huffs of blue-black smoke, while steam from the hard blows
spreads out dirt beneath the trains.

They are falling pealed, piling miles
into why they were born, a flicker
into life's sky—only welcomed home
wearing dust from discarded angels.

Dictionaries are the graveyards of language.
—Simon Dentith

Ephemeral

1. ~~Lasting~~

for a brief time . . .

stand still. Allow me to show
how negligence shifts
in two places. Walk.

Fall off someone's ideas of how
you could have borne some
of their history—

lasting only one day, as certain flowers
or adult insects.

This is Not Our Private Earth

where space begins
                          its field guide
through stars and planets (irregular galaxy)

& the word
when life comes diffused, _____.

As if

purple will be remembered
progenitor red   antecedent blue

truly

it depends on amount
of liquid progenitor-ing:

order spreading
across new-day sky—fireflies find
musk smells on humans
and move away.

Who wants to follow
from

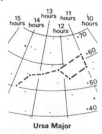

Ursa Major

in order to inhabit

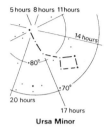

Ursa Minor

Some   find

what becomes   language   vertebrae

out from under rocks conscious

(here it is) headlights on

the ability
to see red as blue   blue that is not quite

headlights on.

Tune   order-construct how

before has ruined—

in one earth
some
are blue that is not quite—

the earth green and blue in parts—

the ownership of thought

no one owns blue   that scours the mind
as some read B L U E—

before
the alignment of individuals' mapping
the scars:

where space begins to individuate
forty-five miles
of nerves   some

have appropriated rights
to the voice that feeds the body.

Influenced   expecting light

this: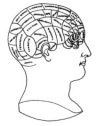

is not our private earth.

We are planets sliced

into ending-blends:

nt as in hu*nt*
nd as in ha*nd*

part   but not the whole—the blend of all things.

————>PUZZLE THIS

8 or 11 leagues behind, thinking
some are so advanced

where we have been made
so-tight-nerves

are all that can shift

posting under street signs

where this:

all that foreplay from the barge,
wanting some strange captain
to come and lead us—

follow who will not lead
(by this I mean dénouement)
is all some claim to have lived in.

By this, I mean veneration
is galaxies barred from days;

in or out makes difference
only to those
                who are traveling in or out.

Unless the map is given in advance? There is more
than one way to West Virginia. The mind is always

traveling   the galaxy unplugs.

By which some feeling is formed   spheres as gates,
spears at the gate

              —some suffer for ways to think;
what becomes

comes out of us.

Take *Nadja, The Dialogic Imagination*

it is good to read books
that think
think upside down

think upside down

learn
a diagram showing location
on the human head of brain—
mindscape-manuscript—

here it is   left-wing-enterprise
order   construct
out of headlights-cliff

an octagon of air blown in
eight sides of breath

it's not even
that some will feel this air
fly through a sweater
and report it differently

it *is*

important to hit a million nerves
for the feeling
of being alive in the body is   expecting

the flight to become us,
have to carry the piano
and build a cockpit out of it   fly

to the edge of every thing——> beat monologic

speed out as bendless miles of nerves.   Write

+70 degrees or 40 can be
within the hour 12   20   or 17
            and then prove

forest   miles around

form.

Let's see veneration, lyrical mind-sign

photoelectric cell, if image
is venue   let's see
your electric eye.

If image *is* emotive of order:

my heart rewinds in inertia,
my mind jungled and Congoed
(the balled-up back of a baby
frittered by lions)—

my soul cheats when smiling

upside down like a reflection

an eye looking into an eye.

As if we are cutting
open a gazelle,
reaching for entangled sinews,
leaving with fists of partridge and wren.

Intermittent (Seats Emptied)

The game is the empty seat.

Stopping and starting
at intervals

the frame is
you are interrupting nothing.

Go on

the long league of tile
toward her chair,

feel the tight-needle-breeze
fan the pit
through the port-bar.

Near an elevator
"in case of fire"

the game goes up
(pausing from time to time)
between fire and living,

as if we all can FIRE
               CALL
               CANCEL
what we have taken

in the storage
of random nights—each person
stepping

trouble-foot

over trouble-foot.

All we have
is
our feet falling in.

We might as well go into rooms
which were not, but wait to become

some small-delicate-precise
where we swim the lengths of ourselves

(it has to be done).

You might as well go
into the game; she

might as well be a cigar.

Into the game she,
you, might as well go—
it has to be done—

where we swim the lengths of ourselves

(some SMALL-DELICATE-PRECISE
which we're not, but wait to become).

We might as well go into rooms,
our feet falling in
is
all we have
over trouble-foot,

trouble-foot
stepping
of random nights—each person
in the storage.

What we have taken,
cancel.
Call

as if we fire
(between fire and living)
pausing from time to time.

The game goes up
"in case of fire"
near an elevator

feel the tight-needle-breeze
toward her chair,

the long league of tile
goes on
interrupting nothing.

The frame is
at intervals
stopping and starting;

the game is the empty seat.

Jasmine Tea

Ready the leaves for reading

so as not to remember

him packing

among gagged and wired chairs.

📖 The Last Few Pages

No one is gone
almost immediately.

Without waiting,

some part of them
hangs around sawed,
dust—without *effort or labor*

father's oak cabinet
is in the Mill House.

The first time
divided earth,

the first chance
to look away
from greater than
or less than light.

Before one has made hands
Before (there is) *time*

to know one's own daughter,

watch storms collect,
throw rain strands
across the bent knuckle
of a porch—*Catch*

what can be lost
at short notice.

And *before long*

come in.

Before the ink (life without
resistance) *is dry.*

Before the fall
in earliness.
Before one's hands
rest and have no davenport,

directly.

Without preparation
(hunter with firearms
shoots through the middle
of a second)
    straight
    straightforth
    straightaway
at sunset
at the eleventh hour

come(s) in—

going out again

airshot
retreats immediately,

4-6 breaths left—
wind spills.

How midnight affords
a lingering wire (a flawed connection
between father and daughter),

give anything
for paces of breath to intertwine,

shoot scuttled blood
across terminal night.

I need him.

His heart
turns through another wire,

radished from form
flogged like oxygen,

one human beat
into light—
retrieve the fire prints.

Walking the leftover leaves through
I have come to understand.

No one is worth collecting
nerveless. I might as well father

some thread
through a marionette,

move the dust
from trailer cars—him walking
the length of that dust and back.

Before This Poem Was Written

I wondered at how
he could not turn around

on Birch St.—*to reduce*
to a shorter form intended
to represent the full form—
(a flowering branch
took me aside) when he was walking

our path. The bells from that church
kept breaking and beating. It was raining there

the water mattered more than our bones.

dif·fer·ent (dĭf′ə-rənt, dĭf′rənt) *adj. Abbr.* **dif.**, **diff.** **1.** Characterized by a difference; unlike. **2.** Distinct; separate. **3.** Differing from others; peculiar; unusual. [Middle English, from Old French, from Latin *differēns,* present participle of *differre,* DIFFER.] —**dif′fer·ent·ly** *adv.* —**dif′fer·ent·ness** *n.*

Usage: *Different from* and *different than* are both widely used,

but the Usage Panel has a strong preference for *different from.* This is especially marked when *different from* can be used without inducing wordiness (when it is followed by a single noun or pronoun or by a short phrase or clause): *This illustration is different from that. This was different from what we expected.* In the first example, only 11 per cent of the Panel consider the alternative *different than* acceptable; in the second only 17 per cent would accept *different than.* But *different than* has wider acceptance, as an aid to conciseness, when the passage that follows is a clause (frequently a shortened or elliptical clause): *How different things seem now than yesterday* (acceptable to 44 per cent). Here *different from* could not be used except ponderously; consequently the alternative to *different than* is to rephrase completely. *Different to,* a third form, is principally British. In an unrelated but common construction, *different* is superfluous: *Three different doctors examined him.*

In the Outline of a City Turned Sideways

Ohio.
The land here has strange furniture;
this one tree, as if movers   forgot
where God wanted it and left it here

among copse
and shinnies.

In hours—roads, history—future will walk
her footprints—firemarch existence. Future
will be quilted into the past like an inferno
of afghans. What if history comes here? I

do

not understand here. Here is not my father;
here is not my grandfather; here is a man from
a nation of hats, whose colors spread across
the desert floor like moonfire. Future walks

through a town
without rumors

memories, or ties. Here is a place where
her footprints are not yet mine. What if I
want to push my veins   back home
where earth crowds, in
mountains, to form a river ↙.
Rivers, the way streets   interrupt . . .
break the . . . uniformity of buildings. We
can walk these streets, the zag-lights, &

h

o

w

well history is the language of what's known
the way what's known goes in the   eternity
of books. What is outside of us: trees, stones
between embankments, & the denominations
of paths finding resistance. Life is not the push, but the rush
alive within us. Catch fireflies in our hands; tell them to blink;
how well our powers remain unarmed. What is held in can witness ✤
it cannot match what fire watches over this universe. All that I
contain within (future flames the present) history is a wicker

f
l
y
l
e
s
s
bird.

The porch is a journey . . .
to travel over or through
past *coup*, present *plume*
future
moon . . . .

Pure Lunch

Her wedding gown is made of live birds
sewn together by their feet,
drying from rain.

To her this is actual; as actual
as the napkins
she has sewn together
that she thinks are birds,

while she stands at the lunch counter
waiting to marry
the fedora in her right hand.

    She would wait for hours
    without eating, sometimes
    without leaning on the silver rail
    by the exit hallway.

Other times
strangers would come, take her
down the walk (away from the customers),

pull her through
red wide doors
    and
sit her on a street
across the walk.

    Her voice becoming moan
    (the sound
    after the shot in the woods),

    fading over

the climb of trees.

I fell to sleep (hearing it)
    and
when I woke   I heard it in my driveway

and on the drive
of machinery at work.

She walked in today.
The chicken cacciatore
was of no interest,
nor the tuna feta-roni.

She doesn't seem to care
what color we are

and if that part that is exotic,
driven toward extinction,

can be evenly folded
in a fresh white box while "gently"
nudging others into place.

She is not the sun
outside of distance.

She is a train
moving into,
then out of a city

far into a galaxy of country,
noticing the scenes.

Scenario

Far into the galaxy of trailer-park geraniums
a few fish eggs hanging out,
thinking

they don't care
what color my life is
or if my vagina will fit anything.

What they care about
is if—in a cosmos of geraniums—
I were one-granulated-dirt-speck

would I want to be close to the stems
or hang out
near the trailer wall?

And
if that matters or not
it could
if one knew (in advance)
if the vertigo cat, who lives next door,
digs in that box every morning.

Mother's Philosophy for Security
(Posted on the Refrigerator Door)

If thieves break into your house
make sure anything they steal
has to be repaired before they can sell it;

& possibly
if the police catch them in time,

it'll be in better shape
when you get it back.

From (with a person, place, or thing as the source, cause, or instrument) the House

For Example

The sky isn't above the house anymore,

must be down here
all the people move like storms.

*
I only meant to tell you
I came home last night.

*
He kept reading

Muscles better
and nerves more

(because I don't want to burden him
I listen).

*
Among the burden of jasmine
        (tea, rare china) burning.

Icarus Falling

The sun cannot rise at a normal time.
It's frozen. On both sides of a highway
brass gates unlock between ice mountains.

Children drop along this roadside.

Dams of gasoline open. Overflowing skin with *eurythmia,*
beneath the road they are running—courage
smothers slowly—into embers.

Matches held by a few men—lit—are let go—*welcome inferno.*

But in between the smoke, the fire shows
a nest of safe arms (we all leap for those arms):

don't go too low, or water will weigh the wings down.
Don't go too high, or the sun's fire will burn them.

Mothers watch, as men gather them—throw them
out of a gate into an avalanche.

I believe

the fatherless form on dust banks.
They form from the leftovers of Icarus falling
as an unhooked worm into sea, hunting
inside the mouths of many fish

for fathers who live
in a foreign country on a foreign earth.

If that is not reality, here is reality:

There was a dust storm on Mars
the day my brother was born,

only his mother was there, in the nursery,
voices break to beat out bells

from the church
near a window by Steven. His fingerprints,
patterns of God living and lonely.

He sleeps while she is reminded
eternity processes us.

In the Absence of E

rwind m mothr
(I am flying backwards in your hands)

rmind m
(the moon falls down   epileptic
kicks its nuisance
across the relay of a fork)

rturn th rasons
(the sun feeling the front porch steps,
all things taken away
like china, the visitors)

rwing m mothr
(make my hands match your hands

epileptic,
kick my nuisance across the relay north

—motion with my arms
so many times, my hands become waves,
take my legs off today)—ralign m mothr

rmov th v
(the e from your pocket-ghost, the other,
then the r from baskets, shell and search
tables their needles—

revive me mother

motion with my arms, another curl in rust
wait as fire dries).

Moonfire

Valley sun and moon arise,
at the same time one thousand
shades of eruption

never before seen in a rainbow
(off-reds, blood purples

mingle indifferent
with carnival green)

step as flowers
across the desert floor.

My mother told me
we were rock of Cherokee, four
pounding gallons of Blackfoot, robbed
from being Creek
for being Irish.

But, she said, *the world
will call you woman;
you will bear the woe
of every man.*

Once I took a look through our valley,

standing on top of a hill, evening rose,
bloomed its way into night-violet.

No matter where the land began to end
there were hills, and a fierceness
within those hills to be named.

My Indian name means moonfire,

a miracle in the desert.

Does language
not give us the right
to rename the pieces of our earth?

Opening the Mouths of Trees

My brother would take me to the river;
we would watch the water around rocks move
hard over stone, push dirt into banks—

on the ground the river walks;
steps across the land in inches, ankles
pulling against earth's urge for retention.

But the world changes in dimension, shadow,
clouds fold over us like the roof
of our parents' house.

(Green walls gathered curtains by the windows. I waited,

the woods outside, the river
like a bending elbow around the land.) Brother's voice
calls water into the ground,
opening the mouths of trees.

It's a good day for rain.
It's a good day—let the world fall down

To the Night River Fish

Don't hit him on the boat, I said.
Look at him puff. He's trying to talk.
Papa threw him back.
                    —Theodore Roethke

You are a fish who believes there is an ocean.

Hunted by yesterday's weapons
you chase your mother's body
into the *huvvus* of burning air,
her breath between two forces—water diving
into noonlit sky.

You are a child, nursing
rapid within her.

You are journey, a cargo
of every man, memories
whose captivity is

any gate
held by soldiers
circling the road.

A roadway trembles into all oceans,
into distance oceans push
between stones.

Speak night river fish
of where the ocean fights that current
for release. Where the tension
from all moving fish
meets the ground underneath.

Live as your mother
in her dreams. As the ocean
swallowing into its belly your river,
as tundra falling into warmer water.

Girl Trapped in Acrylic

> *If there were only one truth, you couldn't paint*
> *a hundred canvases on the same theme.*
> —Pablo Picasso

Here a woman
smudged in purple,
stands before a girl
mangled in red.

Here
I want to trace the border and the line,

tell you she is not beautiful

where her reds are,
& from her blue

the girl becomes more

a girl outlined—

grief that is
as grief does

know someone
simply there.

Here a Room for Hell is

listened to

as if a bombing brigade

could change places with a symphony, rise, then fall into
cadence;

let go of or listened to

as if a symphony & bombing brigade could change thunder

coming in the stratus, rolling

on the night as it fires.

Then live.

Now it is Autumn,

emptying the belly of this land—

the rotting trees herd behind our backs for miles.

Not even time, which hands itself
into a tunnel where there is enough room
for no plans, just leaping.

When we are taken

the way to travel one road
becomes two roads again.

All that history has left

in our pockets

a space too small to put into our hands,

a want too wide to be looked on at one time.

Home Ends

Later, moving statues onto stronger tables, then taking
and sipping cherry tea. It was evening.

What I remember about Thursday is Saturday. Every chair
in the yard for sale, along with others' fingers turning
through a bed, wooden nickels, lead pencils, a riverbed
of chess shirts and blankets, this *souk,* rummaged canisters—"things."

Return the reasons. The sun feeling the front porch steps
all things taken away like china
and visitors.

Kitchen without words, cheese sliced—octagon of swiss, escaping
through tunnels of past days. Time, mercury in her veins (a voice
heard during morning eggs), ancient words in her hands.

Later evening, I went to bed hearing them.

A Story *(A Set of Rooms in Such a Space)*

Introduction to Yellow

We haven't been this frightened since last October

when at Great Elsea's field
we watched gold
pruning the trees—

there were no more magnolias, golden finches,

sand-dusted-marbles
thrown against pewter.

Light blends of heat
stroke (almost) the gray
from flight—

even the geese
have let go of our city.

But we are not *the hue*
of that portion
of the spectrum lying
between green and orange.

We have watched fog dust cleat
the wall of the bridge,

a fidgeting child's hand
let go
of its mother—

want
move lightning into a woman.

And after
she escals to his room, brandied

in the evening

she tries to fly in heat
that wants to be a bird

(& God

did not make her a bird).

We avoid
the changing lanes and guns

among the dam of children's books
(this is not the problem).

We haven't been this frightened
since last October

when
at Great Elsea's field
we watched the gold—our son
left to sleep
under lost dreads of grass.

(What I Want to Give the Reader)
Introduction to Yellow

←—Poetry
goes on this side of the page.

→Writer,
would you like to seesaw in a tornado (fly
in heat that wants to be a bird)?

Yes

(&

I do forget God
did not make me a bird).

Even as I shift

from Detroit
(above news, TV, the crashing
of industry
and flying machines)
into media—

→Reader
I only mean movement,

and how
on a plane
light blends

heat, and stroke
(almost the gray)
from flight

                                        geese
                                          or
                                    cloud-dust

                              moving under a funeral
                                        released
                                   from an engine.

Maybe I am and maybe I am not
the hue of that portion
of that spectrum between
green and orange.

                    I haven't watched fog dust
                        (I haven't watched
                        a lot of "things")

                    move lightning
        into a woman—the color wheel, broken.

                              There never were magnolias,
                              golden finches, sand-
                              dusted-marbles
                              flying against the pewter.

                    We understand:
                        never put

                        a space
                        between

                        the period
                        and the last
                        letter__.

A period
goes
directly
after

the last letter. ⟵

I still
don't want
to do it   .

⟶ Because
it reminds me

of so and so's work,
how s/he did this or that similarly.

(But what does this: ↰ ↓ mean)?

I want readers so
I go on

                avoid the changing lanes
                and guns
                among the covers
                of the dam of library books   **73**

                    (this has never been
                    the problem)   .

I haven't

felt the wind change

the gold (pruning the trees)

thunder coming

on the night as it fires

→Reader

I haven't read art
(in years)

that makes me fly→←

↰ ↓ into heat
(that wants to be a bird)   .

As a Reader

*He developed the theory that Latin poets deliberately
concealed anagrams of proper names in their verses.*

Sir Ferdinand de Saussure:

I have looked
for your name on billboards
near the dam, within the cover
of library books

when Lucretius said: *nam si
abest quod ames, praesto simulacra
tamen sunt illius, et nomen dulce
obversatur ad auris; for if what you love
is absent, yet its images are there,
and the sweet name sounds
in your ears*

.

The way nymphs of the stonefly
evanesce under rocks
to avoid fish culling deep to deep,
I hid in the library near your name

.

I found I could not go:
where the sounds of trains
go into more trains,

to the rumble of forty hogs near shore
and fine piles of sandstone, their recurvation
near the island—where
shots of music
and the launch of fire

could be heard
amidst the carousel's crank
of immovable horses in the park

.

. . . ut nequeant . . .
feraeque inter
sese ullam rem
gignere conveniundo;
and wild beasts
could not produce
a new thing amongst themselves
by coming together

.

Undressed,
aided in air, and
undefined fire is fire,

as far as red unaided
is fire

.

Sir,
I look for your name
(after leaving libraries)
even as thrushes move
against the cubicle of trees (in the foreground),

past porches, alongside riverbeds,
over a bridge,
into a town square

where bent and knuckled furniture
intertwine like squid legs in a dumpster—
how well those chairs remain unarmed

.

And the sweet bearing
of a wheel's sound
against concrete slides
through rain, unaided as fire

.

Anagram from ROCCO NOCERA

```
ROCCO
RECON
AROCC
ECONO
RAROC
CONOC
ERARO
ONOCC
CERAR
NOCCO
OCERA
```

Beeswax! O *cera—candles*
—the shore to the lighthouse is broken. The *ship*
will cart us there alive as fish—*nao,*
nao means its own flesh, broken-dress.

Which in turn will *fray*
*scrape abrade—raer—*us, and we will *fray scrape abrade*
until our stems line up on the shore
in their own fleshbrokendress.

One can care (ROCCO NOCERA) or
no one can care

for how that shore
will *fray scrape abrade* us—

and almost now, I know

Nocera cleans legumes,
rinses them from crickets,
musk trails dust from the stems.

To naked-lake-shore-objects

rain storm trappings,

into the eye of color,
almost a breakable convex
changes the *erotica* of the hydrangea
from a pink to a violent hue.

Even the emotive of order
from English into some said Spanish

cannot make *I like him*
using Rocco Nocera.

A Disgruntled Comment to My Imagination

The woman standing
by the stove
in factory pants
told me not to
make you angry.

But who do you think
you are, telling me
that I can't put you
in any room
on any street?

Here it is Thursday

On the other side of the street
it is Saturday;

room is there
to regard movement, a typhoon
covers the running of a tornado.

In the rhythm of toes
and fine hands, she is dancing;

she is the low cloud
lightning's feet
set onto the earth to march.

I have seen her painting in the museum.
Sometimes
she stands in front of *Guernica*
unable to move;
other times
there is no *Guernica* capable
of the long white flank
crawling toward the venue of lines.

Mountains fall behind in canvas. Voice

journeys into the mouths, their valleys,

the backyard seam of unmade porches.

Surely there is no place she cannot go—

how well those chairs remain unarmed.

                Those who hold her
            stand before life to sing

                find they have no voice
              and refuse to sit down.

              Fabric   sound
              wrap up life and cling.

              She
              is a rainbow underfoot,

the defenestration of color

into the blank afternoon.

(Surely there is some attempt

to travel over her,

but who is within us

cannot change cities.)

We must watch

require inertia   hide walking

know her fire

and hold onto her water.

She is vegetation crooning out

the meter in this city as it edges,

the private earth

leaning through the cut edge

of a horizontal window,

(a conception

of mental creation . . .)

an image, (imagine) the distance

between our houses, its quantity—

what it is to move beyond a concise ocean.

TILERATURE ←start here

The Lane Goes Left; The Lane Goes Right

Metacentre:

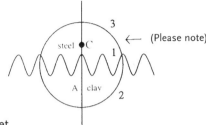

1. Ramble Street
2. The lane goes right
3. The lane goes left

C, center of gravity;
A, center of buoyancy of
a floating body

Please note: the round object herein is Mother's ball

Near a retired cane store a character waits at the red stop—the
red perpetual, a light that never seems to green or yellow-a-go.

Near the retired cane store where a man named Elder
once opened birch to enterprise, and **ESTER'S DINER**
flashes in half-light, the lane goes left, and that lane shifts down
into Eden town, where lights graze the mid-life hour, turning wet
evening buildings into mall alleys. Convalescent children wake
from stone dreams—or never wake.

Time, in each amble, has women and men falling toward
one another while others fumble away from the lane that shoots
left toward *that* part of town; the part of town where time gets
tricked away from people, existence wishes to be leagues of
liquor from light. Here there are needles, viable parkways
driving addicts to their maintenance. The drunk-avengers angel

89

their way toward swords-of-bars, the blown-away-by-gun boys expected.

Here is the lane where women with perpetual lace overtures sing their legs apart over and again; some are found mangled or angled in cars. The kind of women men hook wrist to wrist and then notice things about. It had been So time in So town since she was one of those women men would hook body for body, light for light, that flame falls out of a long white smoke. She would trade the lane for a flame of indigo, somewhere between chemistry and elusive happiness, where that lane sweeps its dismal penumbra around the city.

Character sits at the turn, miles from her bank job, her new apartment. Even without motoring another edge, the wind ricks around her car. Wind sprawls over balcony ledges, lipping the tops of buildings. Through a window, into the house on her left, it flits like dirt clings to braids (woven linen and basket ease) stationed on the counter. As wind moves into the oxygen of hallways and then into bedrooms, where night sleepers exhale in leeward tide, LTM monogrammed on shirts to her right negotiate nothing of the lane, which goes left.

As character edges the middle line, her blue Sierra mugs part of Ramble Street. Which way the lane? Which way leads back to the main road?

This turn is not the beginning. Or the end. Between decision and indecision, the turn is the perfect *medias res* (or meta centre); where the buoyancy of any decision is afloat between the volume of the situation and the weight of the final choice.

This turn is the crumpled orange paper in her passenger seat. Pulled away from the nest of the arm, she holds:

Left on Center
3 Lights
Right on Collier

No mention of Ramble; no "If you pass this diner you've gone too far." No banks. No gas stations for markers (to ask ?'s).

And if there is a Father Time, then who is his Mother: epochs, history? Is she wearing her watch with our 24-hours each? In *the nick of time* giving us *the time it takes*? Does she hold her ephemeral ball of ticks; shake it like a cat toy just before the pitch through times of argument, grief, perpetual mourning, mainstay emotions, happiness, and over-elation from a kiss near the top of a building? Does she not know that character can't tell her son how she got lost until she turns and heads toward him?

Far over from the *bed of embers*—grieshoch—the lane goes right into where the lights of the city kick-still-farther-away, toward big businesses. Here there are towns with twilighted houses that do not have alleys. Where time, which is always lifting, then landing, then lifting that landing (postured in position), limbers up to 3:05, sits impatient—edges a slight fender into time.

Film

Film

How easy
is it for someone
loaded with fire (arms) to control—
an appointed . . . customary moment or hour

for something to happen,
        begin—an experience?

Limited.

The Man Who Brought Her Flowers

When the film began it showed the leaves of a tree. They seemed to be coated with oil, the way they glinted and then refracted light into our living room.

(Cut to . . .)

A woman underneath a tree.

Then the picture opened, and a woman was underneath the tree. She had straight black hair and fair skin, lighter than parchment. She smiled at us in our living room.

(Cut to . . .)

A woman leaned against a tree with her knees in front of her.

She leaned against the tree, knees in front of her stomach, and looked comfortable. Her pink dress with white and dark rose swirls layered in shadow—color over the grass. She leaned over and with small hands rubbed her feet.

(Cut to . . .)

A woman's fingers defined toes as small.

Then she closed her eyes and began to lick her upper and then lower lip slowly and evenly.

(Cut to . . .)

A woman's wild light, and lips being parted.

In the upper left-hand corner of our TV a hand

(Cut to . . .)

Near the woman's face a man's hand

came in holding white and rose-colored flowers. She smelled them, opened her eyes, and then looked toward them.

(Cut to . . .)

The camera pulls back, and there is now a man in our living room (I remember it, as if he were standing in the room, not on the screen itself) wearing brown pants

(Cut to . . .)

The crotch of the man's pants, a crisp untucked shirt.

(Cut to . . .)

A chest behind the man's shirt while he holds flowers. She takes the flowers. Her hands are a little smaller than his. He puts his hand out, and she accepts. They begin to walk toward what looks like a house in the distance.

(Dissolve)

They begin to fade like distance into distance.

Covered for a short time. Father and I sit in the living room. He watches me shove some popcorn into my mouth, then edge my fingers with my lips and lick the side of my hand to get the leftover butter off.

The woman and man come back into our living room and we both begin to watch them. They are speaking to each other. She puts the flowers on an old wooden table. They hold hands as they walk down the canvas of maroon flowers on a cream hallway. He opens a smooth white door and it creaks, but only a little. He gestures with his hand for her to enter first, and she follows his request. She smiles as she enters the bedroom. She doesn't turn around as he gets behind her. His right hand reaches up to the top of her neck, near the zipper, while his left hand is on her shoulder. He drops the zipper. He pulls the sides of her dress off slowly, and then her shoulders and back are revealed to us. She turns to face him, and he moves out of the way so we can see her. With her hands, she grabs both sides of the dress and moves it down to her waist. Then to her ankles.

I had seen a woman naked before this. My mother would let me sit in the bathroom with her as she bathed. I would watch her dunk the pink wash-rag into the pool around her, bring it up, wring it out, and then smudge it with soap from the holder. She would ask about my projects at school, while she scrubbed her elbows, then tell me whose teenage daughter was pregnant at work, or going to prom, and how she dreaded life when I got to their age. Sometimes we would talk about nature hikes we would take in the woods behind our house in November, playing with the leaves, spying colors, and comparing them to fruits: mangos, raspberries, lemons, oranges, and muscadines.

(Cut to . . .)

I don't remember the first time I saw the film. I have seen the film so many times that the memory of what I noticed first, and what I noticed when, is jumbled. I do remember a few times when I saw the film I noticed something else. One time I saw a hint of blue in the leaves of the tree, another time a new glint of light from the left of the landscape. Once, I thought I saw something moving as they walked toward the house and into the distance that herded behind their backs for miles.

(Cut to . . .)

The woman in the film stands before us in our living room. The top part of her body comes close to the screen. Her small breasts look similar to my mother's, like curves of shoulders that didn't quite make it into being arms. (I used to sit and stare at my chest when I would take a bath. My chest was so smooth and flat with two brown dots. I liked my body because it was nothing like my mother's or the woman's in the film.) Her body moves back away from us, and then she stands in our living room from the neck down. She looks like my mother here too.

The man moves in front of her, and he faces us from behind. He is also naked now.

(Cut to . . .)

A close-up of a man's buttocks.

Some hairs stand up like

a bad shave.

I had never seen a naked man until I watched this film the first time. The memory of what shocked me when, and what I eventually got accustomed to, is a thrown-in-the-air jigsaw.

The man pushes the woman onto the bed. She falls back giggling and then smiles. The man comes close to her and puts his knees on the bed. I can see what he looks like. I know I thought men looked strange naked, even more strange than my mother.

The man moves the woman's back and legs into a position that does not look comfortable. Her face shows her discomfort because she grimaces and then begins to move her legs away from him. The man pulls his hand back and brings it down across the side of her face.

(Cut to . . .)

Her eye, and the elephant tear that replaces it.

He yells something. The camera moves itself into its usual position. Slowly she moves her body back the way he had placed her, and he moves his body into her. He seems to be comfortable. He smiles but she has stopped smiling. As her sound begins to carry loudly, he places his hand over her mouth to stop her. He jags his body over hers again and again and her body moves very little. Soon after, his movement stops, he gets off of her and goes to the entrance of the room. The camera takes her away from our gaze. He comes outside of

the bedroom and shuts the door. He is smiling. We are alone
with the man in our living room as he stands there smiling.

    (Dissolve)

   Memory spliced into a thousand separate,
separate parts.

   📖 Father sent me to bed.

   I waited in a chair.

The place where
let down   (motor and point)

becomes
     a wicker, flyless bird.

Frankly—I have—the ingredients:

1 *light air 1-3 mph* *direction of wind shown*

by smoke—not vanes.

   Even the middle of the creation

   (industry to flying machines)

   became a degree,
     a non working alpha (bet)

  2 positions following Z,

    (the beginning)

error—end of resjudicata; he took.
my wrists.

If   (we slip)
wild—body—then

the book will begin:

Woman   make   how   happy

the open fire containing   wall   {Safety nest}

This means   promise/assurance/guarantee

loaded with fire—(arms)

the fraction of a bird
taking off   the rest—

frangible, landing

away from   rupture (body, map)   angle of aberration.

          (this is
          not) End

          of woman with the want of a wilder(ness)

falls—damage is coming ahead—back to

how smoke rises   vertically

(while birds break) into a splendid city—

where rain is never rain but a river   in parts.

What is our matter?   What does not work *sinnishanu*—like women?

                        Come.

Woman make how   to filter <a wicker, flyless bird
happy the open   stop the
fire containing wall   or *at intervals*

               widespread

    damage occurs.

This means close window   (sleep assembled)

slip around contour   the position.

            Or woman (mistook) will fly
            into heat

                that wants to be
           plume coupée—la plume

           tombera. L'oiseau
           tombera unto the end

           the position:

Notes

Greene, Graham. *The End of the Affair.* New York: Penguin, 1975.

Text

"authenticate • automatic autograph": Autographs of Napoleon and Christopher Columbus. ". . . humpback . . ." *The American Heritage Dictionary of the English Language.* New College ed., 1978.

"Miners in West Virginia": Wright, James. *Above the River: The Complete Poems.* New York: Farrar, Straus, and Giroux, 1991.

Dictionaries

Dentith, Simon. *Bakhtinian Thought: An Introductory Reader.* New York: Routledge, 1995.

"Ephemeral": *The American Heritage Dictionary of the English Language.* New College ed., 1978.

"This is Not Our Private Earth": Ursa Major, Ursa Minor images. Copyright © 1981 by Houghton Mifflin Company. Reproduced by permission from *The American Heritage Dictionary of the English Language.* Head of phrenology (head of phrenology dismembered and only parts used from the head of phrenology image; phrenology quote used from underneath the drawing's explanation). *The American Heritage Dictionary of the English Language.* New College ed., 1978

"Intermittent (Seats Emptied)": ". . . Intermittent . . ." *The American Heritage Dictionary of the English Language.* New College ed., 1978.

"The Last Few Pages": ". . . earliness . . . receiving . . ." *March's Thesaurus Dictionary,* 1925.

"Before This Poem Was Written": ". . . abbreviate . . ." *The American Heritage Dictionary of the English Language.* New College ed., 1978.

Different

"Different": Copyright © 1981 by Houghton Mifflin Company. Reproduced by permission from *The American Heritage Dictionary of the English Language.*

"In the Outline of a City Turned Sideways": ". . . interrupt . . . journey . . ." *The American Heritage Dictionary of the English Language.* New College ed., 1978.

From the House

"From": *The American Heritage Dictionary of the English Language.* New College ed., 1978.

"For Example": cummings, e.e. "i like my body when it is with your" Ed. Carruth, Hayden. *The Voice That is Great Within Us.* New York: Bantam Books, 1989.

"Icarus Falling": Ovid. *Metamorphoses.* Trans. Rolfe Humphries. Bloomington: Indiana UP, 1973.

"To the Night River Fish": Roethke, Theodore. *The Collected Poems of Theodore Roethke.* New York: Anchor Books, 1975. The epigraph is from the poem "Where Knock is Open Wide."

"Girl Trapped in Acrylic": Parmelin, Hélène. "Picasso says . . ." London: Allen and Urwin, 1969.

A Story (*A Set of Rooms in Such a Space*)

"Story": *Merriam Webster's Collegiate Dictionary.* 10th ed., 2001.

"Introduction to Yellow": "Yellow." *The American Heritage Dictionary of the English Language.* New College ed., 1978.

"As a Reader": Culler, Jonathan. *Ferdinand de Saussure.* New York: Cornell UP, 1986. Lucretius. *De Rerum Natura.* Trans. W.H.D. Rouse. Cambridge: Harvard UP, 1959.

"Anagram from ROCCO NOCERA": *"cera . . . nao . . . raer. . ."* *Random House Spanish-English English-Spanish Dictionary.* 2nd ed., 1999.

"Here it is Thursday": ". . . imagination . . ." *Random House Webster's College Dictionary*, 1991.

TIJ←— start here
ERATURE

"The Lane Goes Left; the Lane Goes Right": ". . . Metacentre . . ." *Webster's New World Dictionary of the American Language*. New York: World Publishing Company, 1960.

Film

"Film": *Merriam Webster's Collegiate Dictionary*. 10th ed., 2001.

"The Man Who Brought Her Flowers": Words from the Beaufort Scale image. *Merriam Webster's Collegiate Dictionary*. 10th ed., 2001. The word *"sinnishanu"* comes from a journal article in *Parabola*. Conner, Randy P.L. "Men-Women, Gatekeepers, and Fairy Mounds" *Parabola* 25.1 (2000): 71-77.

photo by Steve Davy

Ever Saskya is from Hixson, Tennessee. A doctoral candidate in Creative Writing at the University of Denver, she currently lives in Englewood, Colorado.

New Issues Poetry & Prose

Editor, Herbert Scott

Vito Aiuto, *Self-Portrait as Jerry Quarry*
James Armstrong, *Monument In A Summer Hat*
Claire Bateman, *Clumsy*
Michael Burkard, *Pennsylvania Collection Agency*
Christopher Bursk, *Ovid at Fifteen*
Anthony Butts, *Fifth Season*
Anthony Butts, *Little Low Heaven*
Kevin Cantwell, *Something Black in the Green Part of Your Eye*
Gladys Cardiff, *A Bare Unpainted Table*
Kevin Clark, *In the Evening of No Warning*
Cynie Cory, *American Girl*
Jim Daniels, *Night with Drive-By Shooting Stars*
Joseph Featherstone, *Brace's Cove*
Lisa Fishman, *The Deep Heart's Core Is a Suitcase*
Robert Grunst, *The Smallest Bird in North America*
Paul Guest, *The Resurrection of the Body and the Ruin of the World*
Robert Haight, *Emergences and Spinner Falls*
Mark Halperin, *Time as Distance*
Myronn Hardy, *Approaching the Center*
Brian Henry, *Graft*
Edward Haworth Hoeppner, *Rain Through High Windows*
Cynthia Hogue, *Flux*
Janet Kauffman, *Rot* (fiction)
Josie Kearns, *New Numbers*
Maurice Kilwein Guevara, *Autobiography of So-and-so: Poems in Prose*
Ruth Ellen Kocher, *When the Moon Knows You're Wandering*
Ruth Ellen Kocher, *One Girl Babylon*
Steve Langan, *Freezing*
Lance Larsen, *Erasable Walls*
David Dodd Lee, *Downsides of Fish Culture*
Deanne Lundin, *The Ginseng Hunter's Notebook*
Joy Manesiotis, *They Sing to Her Bones*
Sarah Mangold, *Household Mechanics*